HI-DENSITY POLITICS

Urayoán Noel

HI-DENSITY POLITICS

Urayoán Noel

BlazeVOX [books]

Buffalo, New York

Hi-density politics by Urayoán Noel

Copyright © 2010

Published by BlazeVOX [books]

Printed in the United States of America

Book design by Geoffrey Gatza
Cover art work by Ivelisse Jiménez
First Edition
ISBN: 978-1-60964-031-6
Library of Congress Control Number 2010931948

BlazeVOX [books]
303 Bedford Ave
Buffalo, NY 14216

Editor@blazevox.org

publisher of weird little books

BlazeVOX [books]

blazevox.org

2   4   6   8   0   9   7   5   3   1

B   X

ACKNOWLEDGMENTS & NOTES

Some of these poems first appeared, sometimes in earlier versions and/or under different titles, in *2nd Ave. Poetry*; *Blue Fifth Review*; *Fence*; *Huevo Crudo*; *Letras*; *Mad Hatters' Review*; *Mariposas: A Modern Anthology of Queer Latino Poetry* (Floricanto Press, 2008; Emanuel Xavier ed.); *New York Quarterly*; *Palabra: A Magazine of Chicano & Latino Literary Art*; *The Portable Boog Reader 3: An Anthology of New York City Poetry* (Boog City, 2009; Joanna Fuhrman, Brenda Iijima, Jim Behrle, David Kirschenbaum, Mark Lamoureux, and Paolo Javier eds.); and *sous rature*.

"hidden city" and "uncertain cruising altitudes" incorporate lines from my translations of Osvaldo Lamborghini's poem "'El salvavidas" and Pablo de Rokha's poem "'Pablo de Rokha' por Pablo de Rokha" respectively; both translations first appeared in *Mandorla*.

 "babel o city (el gran concurso)" was composed as a series of minute-long voice notes on a BlackBerry.

"what it's all about" was recorded as a spoken-word piece with music by Monxo López at Spanic Attack's SpA Sounds studio in the South Bronx: www.madhattersreview.com/issue8/audio_noel.shtml.

"a throw of the dice will never abolish south beach," "slogans for the end of the world," and "sitibodis" are free-form self-translations.

 "african noel.coachella valley snow" is a found poem: http://groups.yahoo.com/group/christmas_gifts/message/86.

"me, o poem! (a cameo poem)" is a poem in palindromes.

"the commonest many fester" was staged for six voices (five readers – Roberto Abadie, Guananí Cabán, Martha Clippinger, Demetrius Daniel, and myself – plus software) as part of the Boog Poets' Theatre, curated by Paolo Javier, at Sidewalk Café, NYC, 11 Sep. 2009.

 "the commonest many fester," "sitibodis," and "hi-din sites" were inspired by lines from Rodrigo Toscano, Josefina Báez, and Edwin Torres, respectively.

"trill set" was composed by reciting the first 13 poems from César Vallejo's *Trilce* (1922) into Dragon Naturally Speaking™ speech recognition software. The program's English (mis)interpretations of the Spanish words were then arranged on the page in keeping with the layout of Vallejo's original. As a performance piece, it is scored for two voices, along with either Vallejo's original or Clayton Eshleman's translations.

"guánica" was composed as a series of minute-long voice notes on a BlackBerry, except for the last poem, which was texted as a BlackBerry MemoPad note. At certain points in the Tamarindo Beach section my voice was drowned out by the wind and waves, rendering those portions untranscribable. I have indicated those moments with bracketed ellipses. The text, photos, and voice notes were first displayed together as an installation as part of the group exhibit Panel Discussion, curated by Martha Clippinger, at The Dirty Dirty, Brooklyn, NY, 14 Mar. 2009. For more on Guánica, see here: http://welcome.topuertorico.org/city/guanica.shtml.

Grateful acknowledgment is made to all the editors, curators, collaborators, and interlocutors involved.

A special gracias goes out to Geoffrey Gatza and BlazeVOX for giving this unhomely book a home, and to Ivelisse Jiménez for the hi-density cover art.

HI-DENSITY POLITICS

HI-DENSITY POLITICS

HI THEN (salutation)

Hi then, neighbor! Welcome to the city--
Cool! You're still in time to see the sites!
There's still room in the tourist-trap committees--

All you have to do here is work nights
Up and down the block with your binoculars
Pointing out the billions and the blights--

Someone in a fanny pack is jocular
Watching global banking's clipped collapse--
Theorists put the sexy back in secular

pop art references

While hustling conglomerates for scraps
And corporate def poets workshop street-speak--
Wack oracular? "Yo, IMF raps!"

(Tofutti wraps, that is! Glockavore chic?)--
Ideology is always spite-specific--
(Prefab--beats--to--go--with--your--critique?)

Make poetry less *petro* and more *glyphic*!
Readable as scrawl of city bodies
Fleeting? Or sing, World Poets™ (faux-beatific)

Selling your *saudade* to the Saudis--
We'll stay behind-- globbing up the global--
Mixing *grand mal* Kool-Aid in hot toddies--

Zapping off the statesmen-- Statements snowball--
Spurred by *lo que nunca se traduce*--
Take note: this revolution's temporal-lobal--

I traffic tics then trade up for a loosy--
Altering the chemistry-- (no brainer!)
Seizuring the state-- "O, say, can juicy?"

This anthem's mangled lyrics-- (darned retainer!)
"To re-site the body-- to remember--
To cruise the city-- Lorca meets Joe Brainard"

(Only en *mockspañol*)-- language dis (members)--
Take me home-- city blocks-- I'll sing your chorus
Like an accentual-syllabic punk John Denver--

a poem that is aware of itself

(That was redundant!) Like a Slamosaurus
In its death throes-- hamming it for points--
"I will not add another word" (quoth Horace)--

You can keep the poem that anoints--
That represents-- that narrates or "gives" voice--
Find the voice that *poems*-- that disjoints!

The polis is disjointed (force *and* choice)--
Burn the apartment but keep the complex!
A less Catholic Vallejo or Joyce

Could write my dream with laughtracked sound effects:
All ragged beauty-- provisional-- like struggle
For vision beyond pomo architexts

As ugly-ass as the technocrat's chuggle
That defines us in this cyber *âge*--
Yadda yadda-- The loyalties to juggle:

Art versus community-- glocal triage
(Translocal-- whatever)-- poetry *as* community:
Open-mic-flarf-lyric-decoupage?

The fractious promise of dotcom unity
(e-Bards, bow down before your server!)--
The poetry of trust-fund e-impunity

Or jealousy thereof? Organic Gerber
Poetry to go down nice and smooth?
Or will they listen to this dork unnerver?

I can do my best to rhyme with "soothe"
And when I say "we" I truly mean it--
Only "we" is painful-- we're a groove

Without a nation (we've already seen it--
Thanks)-- besides, our nation *is* the laughtrack
In flight-- (no complimentary peanuts!)--

Confoundational (kick through the sheetrock!)--
Analog-digital diaspora shoutout!
(I'm mixtaping the ipod and the 8-track--

Rocking the identity cutout!)
¡En performalismo está la fuerza!
Forgive the fitful fragments and the layout

And my quirky deployment of the terza--
Quirks like us (the only *us* that matters)--
The glam/glum gleam-- see Kinski-era Herzog--

Who scans the city as it scatters?
Drops the props and scores this scarred propensity?
(The city immeasurable in meters!)

Din of dollar stores-- dust-binned CDs--
Poems living-- breathing-- circulating--
Formal-- neural-- social-- in hi-density!

The poem as a difficult relating
(A city, a polis, and its tics)--
As urgent as the day-- an urgent fading.

"we're a groove without a nation"
↳ BORDER

poem as a city

17

CITY (erode movie)

hi then, city
cooped, recouped
hi-density
hidden
sí, tú
quién?
in situ
our birthright
no
dead end
yet
& then
andén
domainofhope
atdoubtdotnet
a burned
cd
a Citi-®
scan
some ziti
strained
somos sums
cu dada nos
de servers
eros
do shared
sensoria
da citizens
be vocal
dem denizens
transLorcal
say when
ye urb
of quién?

(op. city)

1.born of alarm **2.**Mister Misnomer's *streetform* **3.**against what movement? **4.**daylight again (*carport?*) **5.**parkway searches (*seizures?*) **6.**today's teleprompter monologues **7.**off crosstown bus **8.**to hold on **9.**to the edge **10.**of things (*here!*) **11.**curvature of city **12.**(*slit*) slippage is **13.**the variegated hums **14.**of home and **15.**loft parties and **16.**open mics and **17.**(*slumming slammers? diversifiers?* **18.**assisting the assistant **19.**to the assistant **20.**of administrative assistants!*) **21.**the last dose **22.**of the truth **23.**of man (*whole?*) **24.**the body erratic **25.**retro salsa bands **26.**(*sounds no more* **27.**like tropical trombones?*) **28.**skyscrapers thru clouds **29.**wasted boys and **30.**wilted girls in **31.**drunken lipo limousines **32.**hoarse playa throats **33.**these pancaked pierrots **34.**those (*pseudo?*) wacky **35.**(*faux?*) designer dances **36.**beer nausea stoplights **37.**(*Laforgue's Times Square?* **38.**hydrocephalic asparagus moon!* **39.**[adult?] videos of* **40.**downtowns on fire?*) **41.**spotlight uptown now **42.**language poets already **43.**spoken for in **44.**drab position papers **45.**on the fate **46.**of the city **47.**(*the western Bronx* **48.**is hillier than...?* **49.**big bedroom's chilly* **50.**subway negligee's frilly* **51.**north of Harlem* **52.**means NoHarm dude!*) **53.**where others live **54.**self in other **55.**self as other **56.**fate of man **57.**feat of woman **58.**performance of gender **59.**hipsterpaper of record **60.**classic soul collection **61.**memories of infotainment **62.**in acid-washed landscapes **63.**as intramural cheer **64.**oh democracy now **65.**meet your maker! **66.**highbrow maracas play **67.**anthems of privilege **68.**lowbrow maracas just **69.**keep the beat **70.**middlebrow maracas move **71.**to Canada (*quick!*) **72.**this city isn't **73.**'happening' just yet **74.**just testing! texting! **75.**diabetes supplies language **76.**already spoken here **77.**spoken for now **78.**already a part **79.**of (*collapsing?*) community **80.**let's scorn utopia! **81.**advertisement culture crashers **82.**chorus of stillborn **83.**performers self-help e-books **84.**solitude of night **85.**reclaim the city! **86.**(*from its executors?*) **87.**this reggaetón summer **88.**winter of jackhammers **89.**snapshot synapses: (*vaya!*) **90.**make way for **91.**garbage truck pick-up **92.**up and down **93.**this (*virtual?*) Broadway **94.**where anaphorae pileup **95.**like rat droppings **96.**like corpse cut-ups **97.**like price tags **98.**malt liquor bottles **99.**downed in mixed-crowd **100.**mp3 park benches **101.**telecommunication sector holdings **102.**special-interest laugh tracks **103.**(*failed?*) performance poems **104.**(*forced?*) onto the **105.**page then split **106.**into tercets (*cities?*) **107.**singing now signifying **108.**nothing but flight **109.**back to sleep **110.**now these litanies/unease **111.**(*sic*) of streetlamps **112.**Wednesday mid-week traffic **113.**still backed up **114.**to outlying areas **115.**where the meaning **116.**of "outlying" is **117.**laid bare (*splayed?*) **118.**who pays the **119.**fare for crossing? **120.**always here not **121.**back in time **122.**to the days **123.**before the monuments' **124.**debriefing by brackish **125.**and/or waterboarding pigeons? **126.**Humanoscope® sponsored by **127.**Humania the first **128.**and only drug **129.**approved to treat **130.**dissension in the **131.**ranks of rancor **132.**demographics roughly (*guesstimate?*) **133.**14 to 99 **134.**give or take **135.**a few stragglers **136.**(*a few low-liars? [sic]*) **137.**lower-dosage holograms **138.**of lampoon proletariat **139.**plantation service sector **140.**neocolonial escapades performed **141.**off route n+7 **142.**text exit past **143.**the (*private?*) beach **144.**with (*plastic?*) palms **145.**almost always waiting **146.**to be greased **147.**sad tropics of **148.**discourse at the **149.**misanthropic disco the **150.**tropes of discord **151.**the traps of **152.**discard of dis **153.**this strep these **154.**scarred

armament drives **155.***tú sabes, tipo* **156.***bola global* (*meaning?*) **157.**dead bouncer on **158.**the steppes uncarded **159.**at the border **160.**VIP room (*where/wear?*) **161.**for years the **162.**theorists prayed for **163.**crash for failure **164.**to use the **165.**word "systemic" and **166.** mean it, man **167.**(*in a pinch* **168.***any "emic" will* **169.***do [epid/pand/acad/pol/polys/tot] and* **170.***yet it's hard* **171.***to claim a* **172.***polis [herd? clan?]* **173.** *that's not semic:* **174.**<u>*poetry's pull/duty/condition for*</u> **175.***being written/spoken/staged/marketed and* **176.***horizon of meaning* **177.***its demeaning/diluting and* **178.***somehow it slithers* **179.***across the pages* **180.***and abandoned stages* **181.***poorly mic'd [texted/nexted])* **182.**lang it sings **183.**the meaning's screening **184.**sing! sing! (*I-lungs* **185.***in the scream* **186.**<u>*that is what*</u> **187.**<u>*we are*</u>) fight/flight? **188.**clubby beached wails! **189.**lang sound (*sondas?*) **190.**in the sand **191.**the TV makeup **192.**makeup of nation **193.**the made-up makes **194.**<u>of maids/nannies commuting</u> **195.**<u>to</u> made-up suburbs **196.**where school counselors **197.**watch meta-reality TV **198.**on unmade beds **199.**the litany is **200.**always participatory because **201.**when we become **202.**one with the **203.**tremors we start **204.**moving in sync **205.** with the <u>masses/dem-asses/*demáses*</u> **206.**citizens that came **207.**went and keep **208.**returning day-to-day to **209.**earn and burn **210.**in bakeries shoe **211.**stores banking centers **212.**crammed into a **213.**subway's silver sliver **214.**(*sin ver [so-wey!]* **215.***sin verso? [way!]* **216.***sin verse? [(ob)servers* **217.***(ob)versers])* here/hear the **218.**litany is always **219.**participatory because we're **220.**in sync with **221.**the mutable (*phenomontage?*) **222.**flash by/fade the **223.**technical school posters **224.**with smiling youths **225.**grabbing their backpacks **226.**in well-lit hallways **227.**to stave-off death **228.**slowly (*by degrees/digress*) **229.**"Uh, which wanderlust?" **230.**asks Citizen Wonderslut **231.**to the mirrors **232.**(*yawning... hungover... yadda...*) **233.**a fair question **234.**for mute commuters **235.**(*muttering/huffing shoes untied* **236.***steady stride somehow* **237.***anachronistic already...ahora?*) **238.**superannuated nano onan **239.**city rock steady **240.**flow of passengers **241.**like the plod **242.**of legendary creatures **243.**raised and reared **244.**in faraway savannas **245.**and slowly (*slowly!*) **246.**remembering to speak **247.**limewirerimjob poets post **248.**listpoems in listservs **249.**but I'm here **250.**like an analyst **251.**of assfaults (*whose?*) **252.**crude e-satyr I **253.**like it here **254.**I take a **255.**licking and keep **256.**on ticking off **257.**statistics (*statist tics?*) **258.**you keep Europe **259.**Kant's grounding sudoku **260.**can't remember summer **261.**museums' cupolas and **262.**aqueducts both useless **263.**(*how then to* **264.***sitemize [sic][qué?]* **265.***to deduct one's* **266.***take on downtowns?*) **267.**summer's faded undershirts **268.**cutie being hit-on! **269.**loveseat being sit-on! **270.** oops! laughtrack's gone **271.**you're drunk now **272.** have been so **273.**for some time **274.**will continue to **275.**<u>be so entranced</u> **276.**by language that **277.**<u>can't be overcome</u> **278.**the truth's you've **279.**been around text-blocks **280.**blocking out memories **281.**<u>of semesters spent</u> **282.**windowless qua cubicled **283.**graying grabbing notepads **284.**morning's glyph confounds **285.**you at 3AM **286.**when skin collides **287.**with skin (*scan-scion?*) **288.**you tire of **289.**this nonsense of **290.**detours through cities **291.**answerless again (*throat-clearing!*) **292.**(*"um, clueless proposal:* **293.***let's conflate 'you'* **294.***and 'I'...* become **295.***....underpass to 'us'*) **296.**a litany is **297.**taking shape is **298.**shaking tapeloop socialorder **299.**out to go **300.**blurry disarray of **301.**uptown employees of **302.**will-to-power-lunch (*broker-than brokers!*) **303.**junior executives who **304.**work nights (*weekends?*) **305.**in search of **306.**the lifestyle slogan **307.**the lifestyle drug **308.**the lifestyle lifestyle **309.**spring night (*hoodies?*) **310.**hideous hideouts (*arrivants!*) **311.**sleep in fits **312.**high (*on doubt?*) **313.**sound (*or not-at-all?*) **313.**locked glocal glocks **314.**embraceth transient action! **315.**(*repeateth litany tomorrow*) **316.**voicedform: "a hidden **317.**city's never lit **318.**(*no littoral as* **319.***skylines tend to* **320.***blend distend into* **321.***each others' shudder* **322.***in time to catch* **323.***this simple ring:* **324.***taste the tone!* **325.***stone the state!*

326.*state our truth:* **327.***we're factoid fictions* **328.***making meaning in* **329.***cities enclaves bodies* **330.***pawing slacks mechanically)* **331.**our birthright? flux **332.**we're waiting for **333.**another hard-won breath

I was assembled of billions of clouds, well enough to see my emblem has no rendering, is the thunder of summer.

*

* *

My word is worm-eaten and my heart is full of metaphysical cypresses, cities, moths, laments and great commotions, when the personality howls, brimming with eclipses.

*

* *

I am a composite of elsewheres, since somewhere is an amulet, is ambulance, in a city without preambles-- no sonar in this skylight zone, only the Morse code of frozen dial-ups, of dilated masses, in nodal mode, roaming, from storefront to beachfront, nowhere's elsewhere-where to? Stop.

*

* *

Walking, talking, walking with the earth across many roads, my gestures fall from my pockets, —at dusk I left my tongue at the town square…—, I don't pick them up and there they stay, there, there, like dead birds in the solitude of worlds, rotting; the common man says: "they are sad butts;" and passes.

*

* *

I am addenda of smoke, a silkscreen and a camouflage, my nomenclature's staged, a late-model citizen, between a runway and a catwalk, my bodega bottle now emptied and refilled with poisoned mojito mix so as to drown the downtowns and remake them in the name of all my nameless neighbors; in this time of frequent flier friendly fire, border crosser boardroom crises, no cast and clause completes me, only the echo of impossible language, impassible, impassable, the answerless query of the day.

*
* *

Yesterday I believed myself dead; today I affirm nothing, nothing, absolutely nothing, and, with the cosmopolitan feather duster of anguish, I shake the cobwebs from my skeleton smiling in the gray of skulls, of paradoxes, of appearances and thoughts; like a snake of fire the truth, the truth bites lugubrious Pablo in the ribs.

*
* *

Why do pleated beige slacks still exist? To give the off-white collar workers in my neighborhood a reason to believe-- in crossover, in nation, in a home after ruin and a reason for being-- no longer undocumented in this expanse of lo-rise highrises.

*
* *

My anguish and my belly scratch away at my songs, with the hairy and sinister claws of infinity; I'm going to abort a world; (my underwear, my underwear roars with laughter!).

*
* *

Dónde está? Dónde has estado? Haz estado. Estado hoz. Sin mago. Agotado. Hago estado. Make state. Make statements. Meant to unseat powers. To unmic the static. To let loose yr. loosy revolution on these streets, distritos, discrete ethos, secrete us, secret estados, esta dosis by decree, the cry, desisting.

*
* *

A blue coffin and some senseless, intermittent songs guide my worldwide strides.

*
* *

A kind of marine animal, I, attuned to the morning, the mess, working through the enigma of cognition-- hidden city, you were it, and it was spring, meaning perhaps you were the spring in me, the sunlight and the withered trees, idem eyes, sediment smile, see me through; the lull of cities ends here, in your hi-density, your synapse, the distance between skin and sky.

*
* *

And the lice-infested blanket of life wraps grotesquely around me as light does to the blind... (Stir of multitudes, automobiles, crowds, going with me; like a lonely and crazy bird the absolute sings in the black poplars of your head, Pablo de Rokha!..). (—... ... ... Universe, Universe, how we go fading out, Universe, you and I, SIMULTANEOUSLY! ... ... —).

babel o city (el gran concurso)

(Joyce Kilmer Park, the Bronx, 8/06/09 - 3:41-4:27 pm)

no identity   but in hi-density   proximity of buildings   of bodies   more than proximity   a propensity to shudder   when faced with   the other   in self

it's not about   recognition   anymore   not about visibility   or the viability   of discourse   the struggle   and its accurate   representation   the word undoes   the terms of accuracy

what do I mean   by the word?   let's start with   sound   as in   bus exhaust   pigeon squawk softballs plunking   crying and calling

the body's never   simply instrumentalized   roar of jet or taxi in between   what kind of access can we have   never immediate   only instrumental

the machine I read into   makes the most of breath   as shared   it props up   the experience

all politics is tics   therein the polis   all agitprop is props   fed through gadgets   sunscape matters   inasmuch as shared   summer matters   inasmuch as shared   a city is always   inasmuch

this park could use   some garden mulch   the kind that's spread   by old guys in riding mowers in midday cable ads   this park named after   the poet of "Trees"

this park   with the Lorelei that spouts   to hip-hop beats   has done well   with its trauma   has survived the compression   of urban space   and its latter day   reopening   to families and markets

for long this park   bore witness   to a city of markups   no Marxspeak poetrybuzz could undo perhaps now the city is   remarkable   in these unstable markets

turning back into itself   even as it welcomes   beckons   as it has for 200 years plus   a poetics of plus   hard to come by these days   we've grown too placid   flaccid   too easy now   to groan: *"that was a good one, bro!"*   is there any other kind?

a poetics of   kind-of   approximate like Tzara   the neurons' kindling   in hi-density   the boulevard's bus lane   in hi-density   the bodies organized   in hi-density

poetics of opening   are always   optimistic   beacons in the mist   in ways that   collude with markets   collide with careful   modes of criticality   the kind that I   should traffic in

except that   I'm concerned   with another kind of traffic: strophic   no trophy in   this
dystrophy   yet this   is all we share   maybe enough

turbines overhead   where are   we propelled to?   towards meaning   perhaps   to speak   is to
insist   on meaning-making   against the body's   unmeaning

no density except   in hi-density   no resolution   except   in dissolution   the airplane banner
advertises banking   too late   but just in time   for the Red Sox game

that's right   I'm on the Concourse   Yankee Stadium   overhead   the slurp of a tamarind
snowcone   overheard

are those tourists   on their way   to the Bronx Museum?   certainly not local   (but then again
neither am I   still in transit)   clearly out of place   in this enclave   of black and brown

of art deco   and reggaeton dembow   scooters and scatters   some skaters too   but none of
that   quite matters now   it's what I   mutter here   my own meter   muted

I guess what I'm   asking is   can I be a   spokesperson   when all I have are spokes   jarred by
transit   years away from home   can there be a   body politics   in the digital era?

is there a liveness   to this hive   in archive?   can a lone voice   score the tribe   or its own scars?
at least describe   the fractures   and the flows   can meaning   grow from here?

grin and bear it   if you can   the din of cities   and if you can   well wear it well   make sense
of where   unsettle belonging

like   is that a John Deere tractor   running down the Concourse?

yes it is!   likely   on its way   to new construction   new constriction   of urbspace   Lorelei   can
only watch   this isn't   Kilmer's Concourse   after WWI   comes two   to too tú   comes
opposition   depositioning

politics now   is all about positioning   we know that   so far   from the greatest   generation
down with   generations   in their place   iterations   soundscapes   body scrapes   a voice
somehow   between the Skypes   and the skyscrapes

ok   so call me out   I'm an unscrupulous   developer of meaning   of forms   call me   the
Robert Moses   of bad BlackBerry verse   is there a modern   project still?

in these provinces   of voice   not simply projective   these projects around us   my introjective
turning   my trajectories   as a child of colony

empire makes us   instruments   and I'm   a function of one   no CDs   no more   no DVDs

29

no need for them   divided   in our articulations   what we have

are nations of   niche markets   propped up and   held together by   tech instruments
rudiments of communication   no unique   no common

we're all   newcomers to this   and yet   we feel so old   striving for   a purer sense of   presence
those pigeons   don't bark   neither do   those rat-like squirrels   they overtake   the park   a
whorl of tails

they claim   the territories   as we constrict   back into speech acts   seeking out constructivist
potential   in our bodies   shared in cities   by turns   jumpstarted   and art-marted

getting carded at   social clubs   somehow empty   all the time   there's such   solemnity   in my
gesture   such piped-in   pathos   in my voice   how many pesos   would you put on this?

I'm weighted   my own   gestural economy   shot   my formal choices   forced   rehearsed
however live   (airquotes airquotes)   mine is   a poetics of constraints   mine   it ain't

no mining   in this era   we're undermined   by citing   a sudden setting   of the sun   over the
Concourse   at 4pm   the rain this summer   the endless gray   the gruesome succession   of
stalled subway cars

wannabe Beat   Nuyo   New York School   redundant   thankgod school's   out for summer
thankgod Alice   doesn't live here   anymore than   three days a week   maybe four

before   I shut this down   I have to ask you   am I coming through   am I making   sense   in
this economy   of unmaking   of positioning   is meaning to be   made at all?

maybe   just found   semi-pro found   all meaning is   positioning   phishing schemes   pop-up
scams   and the most   radical   thing you could do   vis-a-vis politics   is to call   these tics   by
name

to document   my seizures   not just   my searches   and the struggles   of my neighbors   but I
don't have   the heart for it   the courage   I'd much rather   scat   into the box   tap into   a
meaning that's built-in   sidestep the certainties   of skin

and share it   with the few   who filter through   the laughtracks   and work their way   through
the wound

POLIS (pop lists, oulipolips)

IT'S ALL ABOUT THE SLIGHT LIMPS, BABY, THE ETHNIC FOOD THE QUEER RAZA THE SITUATIONALIST THEORY THE MECHANICAL BULLS THE INCA TEMPLES THE LEATHERETTE GLOVES THE STIRRUPPED CUTUPS THE BAD BEATITUDES THE STILLBORN MORNINGS THE PARTIAL MEMORIES THE UNDERWEAR HANGOVERS THE S&M AT THE H&M THE SLUTTY STUTTERERS THE COOKING WINE THE MISSIONARY DROOLERS THE SIMULTANEOUS SUBMISSIVES THE SPOKEN WORD PERVS THE BROKEN DOWN NERVES THE KINKY HICKS THE NERDY RICANS THE DIANA ROSS DERRIDEANS SINGING *BABY, BABY, WHERE IS OUR LOGOS?* THE OFF-KEY HARD-ONS THE OFFHAND COME-ONS THE SPURT THAT HURTS THE VAGUELY IRONIC FLOWER SHIRTS THE BEARS AND TWINKS THE FAILED ART PUNKS THE TRENCHCOAT GROPERS THE LAPSED INSOMNIACS THE LISPING MANIACS KNOCKING AT THE DOOR OF BELLETRISTS THE GRANNY GROUPIES THE LANGBANG JPEGS THE ONES THAT STARE AT CEILING FANS WITH EMPTY HANDS THE OUTER BURROUGHS AND INNER GINSBERG THE INABILITY TO SPELL THE L WORD (WITH ONE'S TONGUE) THE POLY-CURIOUS AND BI-AMOROUS THE ACNE ACADEMICS THE UNKEMPT MARXISTS THE EXISTENTIALISTS WHO, WELL, EXIST THE SEXLESS EXES STILL OWING IT THE UNFIT CITIZENS WHO SNORE AND SIT THE JERKING POOR WHO KEEP HEROICALLY JERKING IT THE DEF JAM DEFICITS THE STAND UP FAILURES THE REVOLUTIONARY SPAM E-MAILERS THE ONES WITH FUNGUS THE FREAKS AMONG US WHO NEED NOT SAY IT THE TRIPE-SOUP-TYPE THE PORK-RIND-KIND THE BUS PASS HUNCHBACKS THE IMMIG/RANTS THE BALDSPOT WEARERS THE ONES WHO STUMBLE ON THOROUGHFARES THE FLÂNEUR KINFOLK THE LAUGHTRACKED DIFFERENCE THAT'S LACED WITH DOUBT THE WHATSIS

POUT THE SUM OF SOME WHO ARE NOT THE SAME AS THE SUM OF FULSOME OTHERS AND THEIR MOTHERS WHAT'S *PAST!* WHAT'S *OUT!* WHAT'S *PASSED OUT!* WHAT WE *DOWN WIT!?* WHAT THE *UNLIKES* LIKE!!!

east village conviviality imperatives

(*downtown, 2006*)

East Village

Million Heiress

Shaken for granted

Lycheetini mainline

Been recalled

Chai smiles

Sticktoitiveness

Interpretive dance with daggers

Tompkins mohawk'd pooches

Nostalgic for big hair days

Real bohos

Immigrants on stoops withstood

To claim

Q: Post-millennium?

Against '90s reclaiming

Courtesy of mullet

Peace corporate

ISBN

The worth of words

As is!

Must!

Maraschino stem systemic

Socioaesthetic emporium called "downtown"

(or being so)

Topped with can-do attitudes

Post-it artistes play post-aerosol tag

Dull sun

Hip-hop goths given to waxing

Days when there were heroes

CBGBs stood

[with whom?]

[for what?]

A: Culture as claiming

Eminent domain hosting provided

Incestual complex

Etruscanner

…y usted?

[for trades, for laughs]

very of its moment

What's wrong wit dat

No exit

Wine and cheese

First K-Mart

Audiences with arms open

Bringing it all back

"Rise up East Village!"

Post-faux

Mixed drangs

Convivialitinis

Vermouthings

[data entry of the future]

Museum cupola leak

Receptionists

[and after art what came?]

Untenably clothed + retrocoiffed =

The straphang songs of yesteryear

[perhaps in jest]

Tuneless tunes

Display case cutups

[overheard]

[not yet stirred]

(chorus + soliloquy)

"the people's poet has left the building"

INT. A downtown supermarket.

CHORUS: grotesqueries of frozen food { } the check-out counter Publix { } afternoons buried in BlackBerries { } as another ice shelf budges { } job candidates with wheeled luggage { } have stopped to hear the street poet's sermon { } the one about the jackhammers { } the fratboy beatbox { } the box wine kegger { } the trivia trap { } the one about the fading of the page { }

EXT. A toll booth near the city limits.

CHORUS: the turnoff to the x-urb { } the x that marks { } cracks in borrowed sociolects { } *"SUBU FUBU!"* { } who can endure the streaming media { } burrowing jets? { } the Sacher moms { } come to watch the Dobbsian ferry { } drown { } a pimped-up Prius { } Ameriprise rider crash { } headless like the monuments { } sphere not the Publix { } *"knot here"* { } stands out by the highway { } *"sweet!"* { } where sidekicks are discarded { } each road replete { } where migrants hang { } like fuzzy dice { }

EXT. A rest stop convenience store.

CHORUS: beaming signals by the on-ramp { } the chloroformalism of the suburbs { } more pageant tweens { } the moon is law { } it calls the ghosts by name { } the gleam of gas cards { } and Circuit City's remnants in the distance { } the meteoric low-rise { } the mired denim { } in the air-conditioned caverns { } by the cranes { }

INT. A shopping mall food court.

CHORUS: oligarchically they stammered {   } something about bail out and merger {   } BDSM communities keep propping up {   } in bedrooms and boardrooms {   } across the middling corporate climes   {   } mid-list communities still desirable {   } available as on-demand {   } as-is {   } as if the statues stood {   } a chance of trading up for marble countertops {   } too late to counter Publix {   } the formidable formica {   } the expanse {   }

EXT. An uptown fire escape.

CHORUS: here {   } what the city of dreams looks like {   } piecemealed into the possible { } its settlers once so resolute {   } now omniplexed {   } by the HDTV-nativity of it all {   } face the knee-deep masses {   } with their own folding chair polity {   } safety is a gift {   } if we dare die for it {   } say ourselves elided {   } it's rue-e-nation time {   } another Wiki-weekend {   } under fire {   }

Dissolve. Fade in.

INT. An empty open mic.

SOLILOQUY:

I've never bought it
I've never bought that we're anything other than buying
when we drive by the storefronts and deface the mannequins
with "Fight The Power" graffiti

{laughter}

We're always moving
always missing our reflection
in abandoned public park fountains where we used to congregate
still do
still congratulate each other on survival
on *"Viva la ciudad y su cianuro!"*

{applause}

To die now would be paramount

so say the terror horoscopes
be tantamount to calling this umbrage what it is   {nodding}
remembering when folks wore unironic clothes
wrote manifestos
and fastened their illusions to the world
provisionally
in always improvisatory fashion
with the unrepentant grin of failed nations in their shadow
                                                                   {cough, sip}

Because today the summation of the West
has come to rest here in a park bench
in an ex-urban planner's brunch-time playground
where conversations pan quarters
span revenue streams of square footage:
the Avenue of the Parvenus
is being rebuilt again
with gilded silt... all Gehry-rigged
with online promo promises... the webstreams drone
unaware that around us people speak brown French black Spanish English blues
every possible coloratura, you dig?
                                                                   {"hell yeah!"}

But I digress...
I die... I guess...
"the West is caving in" say the headlines
the headless shockjocks and sockless CFOs
epoxy lips claiming God's proxy
bloodletting meets subletting
parceling the bandwidth
chroma keying constituencies...
...you see señor?   "Sí saw!"
Besides, isn't it clear to them that caving in defines us?
                                                                   {spotlight}

We, ahem
a function of collapse
of YouTubed Activia ads
free verse mortgage
speedy delivery... who posts the clips?
Who clips the lampposts en route to the edge of town
past 99 cent stores and freeway turnoffs?

Another American Expressive signaling the fade routes of e-commerce...
Throw your Kangol hats up in the air
and take off your American Apparel guayabera!
This new urb will not save us!
(Save for a rainy day trip.)

There is a city here
hidden in plain sight

{the choir claps a rhythm track,
fist bumps, curtains}

rhythm amazing

(Crown Donut, 161st Street, the Bronx)

syncopated playing in the park   down by the apartment with the drawn curtains   where immigrants are born and die   solos in the twilight ether   sounds askew the neighbors downbeat   the orle the garland   synapse and starlight   the perfect score to the streetlit teleplay stowed in garbage trucks   the all-nite donut countertop spot check   pass the mic and live thru the murder within   sidewinding the bum note   how's everything?   security no homeland never better why?   reality check cashing   cash only realty   dead in the city   they wouldn't have made it   families in freefall   shy boys like tombstones   in fluorescent diner   somersault I/quotidian We   no nation in pronomination   assertoric flow/flaw   adult diapers on cable   he who has E.D. needs G.E.D. needs G's   is spotted trained to kill the impulse within   to overload the shopping cart   to flood the express line with price check items   voided coupons as afternoon gives in to cruising eyes   *AAAA*   "Love to Love You Baby"   fun while you wait to decompose   daily on premises   the face in the mirror   stage dive creosote babies   bound by the variable   rate of deception   I speak of the self and its limits   its mullet phase   its postindustrial complex   unserviceable sector   invisibility TV now comes with wireless   with no comes a where to   multidimensional   mass movement unmapped   could never be captured in tekne   the hackneyed delivery   the wack flow   still blows away the week-kneed audience incipience of/and/as community   the only kind   the rest is special interest focus group granola subprime midnite madness at the drive-in pixelation fest   nomad daemons emailaise   whatever its foibles I tell you the city still swings/seems/fumes   the highrise imposes   the diner odorizes diasporan flâneurs   the 80s freestyle still oozes from overlit clothing stores   "Forget Me Nots" still plays at least four times per day on the dance station   as does "Le Freak"   *AAAA* communities of saturation   iteration stops not later on Saturday   the store-bought beauty of want and dream   and busted hustle and bus stop breakups   angry-assed repentant or simply pent   and who killed the republic? say the bells   whose public?   sad futuric bells   fidget with the grim/the grime/the word   whose sad chapel?   tolls for us its cavernous enormity   enough of intimacy   i'm into my city shared   pensive expansive   we're still here   all of us citizens of din   denizens of now   many-festooned destiny in songs   always about to forgo

On the plane from Argentina
Reading Lamborghini
An Argentinean poet
Born the same day I was
The same year as my father

Lamborghini like the car
Lamb or genie?
Who's to say---
Pet him and see

I couldn't say no to you, that "no...o,"
because I'd gotten close to you: like so,

O. Lamb lived in bedlam
Died (in bed?) in '85
Embedded like I am
In lang itch

He wrote about incest, bestiality, pederasty, literary theory
& pulled glossolalic glocks
On the suburban streets of our semantic cities

He drugged, fucked (Did? Was?),
Died in Barcelona
(In bars? A Loner?)
(With scars? A boner?)

And over the years: how many will have ridden me
while, old, you lost your access
to the sea

My favorite verse of his is

   (SHUFFLE THROUGH *SELECTED POEMS*)

_____

"Me niego totalmente a escribir en mi lengua"
(Chosen at random: "I totally refuse
To write in my tongue")
Notice the italics---
But aren't all Argentines Italics?

Lamborghini vroom vroom
He goes well with the
Swell smell of verbi
celli
maggoty aftertaste in Osvaldo's
angel hair

And I didn't compare you to the Greek gods
(I steer clear of such foolishness).

His poems read like fake diary entries
sort of like what you're reading
now, nao, não
psychoanalytic
casting couch confessions
bad literary theory
good B-movie dialogue
same thing: the mother,
hysteria,
            naked goddesses,
hung lifeguards,
                        wordplays,
lurid days in warped daze in
an oversized haul
and dais

And well,
and now, the prison queens will have a ball.
Which ain't the same!

his shit was real primal
but then again whose shit isn't

[PEEN – ya]

[ah – TAH - ree]

FRENCH

un coup de dés jamais n'abolira south beach

LA TELE-ANOMALIE

la confusion des familles solennelles en face de la télé en regardant le néant métonymique d'une âge post-mythique

LES EMBLEMES DU SAVOIR

et se savoir ravi par la vérité de l'autre
d'hésiter au matin plat de l'agonie quotidienne
le télémarketing avec sa bande sonore des sourires décaféinés et un terreur modulaire

LE MOT ORIGINAIRE

dans la bouche d'un corps déshabillé de sens   des rythmes   des sons tons   symptômes d'une interconnectivité fétide

a throw of the dice will never abolish south beach

THE TELE-ANOMALY

the confusion of solemn families in front of the TV watching nada as metonymy of a post-mythic age

THE EMBLEMS OF KNOWING

and knowing oneself sold on the truth of the other
of stalling in the glum morning of workaday agony
telemarketing with its soundtrack of decaf smiles and a modular terror

THE FOUNDING WORD

in the mouth of a body stripped of sense   of rhythms   of sounds tones   symptoms of a rank interconnectivity

Face à qui
on se met à prier,
à transcrire la dévaluation du douleur?

Face à qui
l'occlusion des paroles,
la chute des projets communautaires?

CITOYEN QUARANTAINE!
Qu'ran//Teen // Yen //Op cit //
CITOYEN GARNISON!
Garniture//Gare //Nation //

Où sont vos frères?   En cherchant des provisions dans la côte d'Angleterre?

Et à la fin tous réunis aux États-Unis dans une plage sans nuages?

quasi//presque//simili...

MIAMI!

In whose face
will you start to say grace,
to transcribe the devaluation of the dullards?

In whose face
the occlusion of words,
the failure of community projects?

QUARANTINE CITIZEN!
Qu'ran//Teen // Yen //Op cit //
GARRISON CITIZEN!
Garnish//Garish //Nation //

Where are your bros?   Spitting rhymes on the white cliffs of Dover? Wack floes!

And at last reunited in the U.S. of A. on a beach where the plastic palms sway?

quasi//almost//could be...

MIAMI

prose poetry?

David noel 34 of christmas party ideas for a crowd school not petersburg buffaloes and noel and 1950's christmas catalogs or african noel of garland county taxes. Noel sites in french or paintings of noel halle of c est noel car il neige dans ma tete of angel christmas tree ornaments + religious + maché gown not al green first noel of ecards free gay egreeting cards uploading own pictures. Noel lemmings not judy garland - biography or noel coward audio london pride not snow boots in australia and christmas decorations outdoor noel candle of christmas halographic lawn train set decorations. Nancy noel graphics and free small shelf sitting bean bag snowman patterns of noel jones standup and literacy programs in santa barbara or noel en provence and wholesale novelties christmas. Ozark trail northpole tents not dr. seuss how the grinch stole christmas cartoon or chris noel or why do people sing christmas carols on christmas of noel gift and dont you wish your girlf! riend was hot like me. Sing noel lyrics of saved by the bell game not grandeur noel company or book with manhiem steamroller music and noel pearson + my boy or twas the night before christmas laugh belly shook bowl. Noel hall and fred hammond-more more more or deer lawn ornaments and noel paul stookey + unitarian of where does the santa fe trail not first noel song not garland texas medical clinics. Noel gallagher and morrissey not make advent calender and wreath of jonathan brody noel coward of salute your shorts lyrics not christmas noel or faery kingdom. Brenda lee + papa noel of heat miser snow miser snow globe not noel ware and marian high school or snoopy , charlie brown christmas or ian noel attorney at law of original instruction manuals bell howell 8mm projector. Nancy noel studios or chicago cubs winter of discontent and noel christmas cookies or winter break camp francisco of listen first noel by clay aiken not driver for a pixie monitor model dl-1455m. Puppete! er noel macneal or sweden culture and traditions not noel house seattl e not snow white the seven dwarfs halloween costume not cantique de noel mp3 not beauty pageant sunburst. Art director noel haan or catherine bell nude photos or picture of papai noel of ideas for family christmas gifts of santa around the world collection by grandeur noel or u.s. gold medal 1998 japan winter olympics. Noel wellborn basketball camps or wedding traditions in france and noel ignatiev biography not pictures of edmonton's snow of still enchant me noel coward into the vortex or abba - happy new year. Noel m. tichy or elk christmas tree ornament of noel holub of snow white samira in bild newspaper and bitter sweet noel coward script of art deco christmas cards. Ginette rino - pere noel arrive ce soir or snow shoe resort wva. not video of the noel edmonds countdown gotcha of speak bengali of noel group and us womens gold metals in japan winter olympics. Songs of noel gay mp3 and blue delft twelve days of christmas plates and noel carte not directions for a baby ! diaper wreath not noel flohe of jessica simpson's video for let it snow. Noel brissenden yegian of radio broadcast of the christmas story with 3 gay wisemen or free electronic text the blithe spirit noel coward or advent calendar house of pornstar stacy noel not how the grinch stole christmas lyrics. Noel lloyd review or hand made greeting cards by artists not northpole mobile furniture not life spa garland texas or noel christmas or vietnamese new year. La nuit de noel not the christmas store wisconsin or shannon noel missouri death penelty or erica adams louisiana pageant not noel callahan or winter vacation packages,ontario. Ding et dong pour noel and free kids christmas

games or rene noel complicated and chris noel uso or david noel gallery not bulletin boards of christmas childrens art. The first noel classical guitar tab and santa baby chords not noel christmas show and snow mountains in lord of the rings or 1956 noel coward comedy or congratulation letters at! work birth. Santa claus at the northpole and san and francisco and cr oss-dresser and christmas and party not nancy noel studios not grinch ornaments not dave and sandy noel of pictures of santa in other countries. Noel lloyd middletown, pa of appalachian symbols, customs, traditions of christmas or france marches de noel not start up business and greeting cards of nancy noel angel prints not new years around the world. Where the girls are 1967 tv noel harrison or ornaments for christmas tree not noel edmonds gotcha or cranberry christmas decor and history of carol the first noel of island of the misfit toys sam the snowman. Musique de noel and oakmont santa rosa ca california new construction low income of crash test dummies the first noel and 2005 winter weather forcast or nantucket noel information and free christmas wallpaper christmas wallpaper. Noel m. tichy and santa clarita mustang and noel coward lyrics not manchester parties for christmas of compagnie coloniale noel or santa claus hat. David noel in van buren ak not winter storm 20! 05 or magnetic northpole of boise, id: winter activities or naughty noel password not christmas cards for a cement business. Northpole to south pole, miles or winter survival first aid kit of marches de noel not the winter soldiers of brenda lee + papa noel not map of santa clara wineries. China pearl noel 64 pc set not southwestern bell telephones or grandeur noel collector edition 2004 not leather santa claus belt and noel coward and short stories of boy as girl in a pageant. Noel arms hotel, chipping campden of santa monica beach cam or noel w. lloyd of catalog on fairies and costumes not noel devine and barry sanders not funny fairy tales three billy goat gruffs.

ME DO MODEM

LOAN AOL

EL GOOGLE

¡EMAILÍAME

MI I.M.!

WWW

TODO.DOT

SU TO-DO.DOT.US

MOCO.COM

ODE I.M. SONNET: *¡TENNOS MIEDO!*

E-Z! I *LA BOLA* LOBALIZE

DELL APPALLED

MAC[E].CAM

GATEWAY A, WE TAG!

NOT/E/BOOK O! O! BET ON!

LAPTOP POT PAL

CODA.DOC

iTUNED ODE: NUT, I

LET NIX INTEL!

NOR ELECT CELERON!

K.O.! O! BE CAFÉ FACEBOOK!

E.DOT I//MOVEON.OBAMA.BONO//E-VOMIT ODE

ZERO! O! PROG OR POOR? E-Z!

E-RICIN! AGRO-ORGANIC IRE!

VIRAL, O POLAR I.V.!

ONLINE.NIL.NO

GOOOOOOOOOOL!!!!! BLOOOOOOOOOOG!!!!!

O.S.! SO?

TUNE.NUT

palíndrome

FLARF.FR! ALF!

(GROG!) ALIEN ONE, I LAG (ORG)

LANG IS SIGNAL

MAP SPAM

CC:BCC:

KUMAR! ROM OR RAM.UK

DAOLOAD

YAHOO…*HAY?*

PHAT, *SÍ?* VISTA HP

BE.WEB

TENDON@NOD.NET

CROW.ORG

SUE.US

VOGUE@EU.GOV

[AS U.S.A.]

NUMB IBM U.N.

SET AGE: GATES!

O SOFT *FOSO*

MIC I.M.

DO PISS iPOD!

MP3@3PM

NOON

NITE…GET IN!

DELL U. DULLED

E.DUD, DUDE

NET@FLIM, MILF@TEN

E-FILM LIFE

REBUT U TUBER

[SIC] [IS]

NOMAD DAMON

HELM THE HTML, EH?

IF I WI-FI

BEWARE ERA WEB!

RE: VERSES…REVERSE, SR. EVER

SERVER…REV…RES

I'M AN "I":   A MOD DOMAIN AM I!

[*This is a playem: or team play/poem. One team is responsible for each column. The player on the far left begins by reading the first line for Team A, another player then does the same for Team B. Play proceeds from left to right, each player reading one line. Underlined lines are read in unison by the entire team. At the end of the poem, the whole process is repeated in reverse, starting with the player on the far right and ending back on the first line. A capitalist version can also be played, wherein individual performers receive a score, as in a poetry slam. Anarchists and situationists are free to reshuffle or improvise.*]

Team A

We be Engels
You be mocks
What's wrong widdat?
We be angles
You be merch
We be angler
You be mangling your remarks
We be Mindy *and* we be Mork
You be sprinkled with remorse
We be languor you be snark
You be bunglers, manglers
You be Bangles to our Bach
What's wrong widdis?
You be Ben Gay to our shorts
Now dissis wrong!
Disses!
We be shingles on your smirks
You be morgue-light to our sparks
Dat's low!
We be bongos make you march
You beleaguered IV Leaguers
You top-down-pun-krock-bottom-
      feeders
You be Horkheimer to our Adorno
You be door-climber for our hot porno
You be flawed primer of our Inferno

We represent ourselves!!!!

Team B

We be Marx
You be men-girls
What's wrong widdis?
We bespangle
You besmirch
We be shark
You be Merkeling your remains
We be Pringles in Mork's mouth
You be Spenglering in dis murk
We be lingering on a lark
We be tinglers, tanglers
What's wrong widdat?
You be bingo to our sports
Now dat's wrong!
Dices?
You be bramble to our bark
We be shambles to your parks
You be Wal-marts without red-lights
The lowest! Guaranteed!
You be pagers for dem narcs
You belabored labor leaders
You uptown-frontin-crunk-lite-
      breeders
You be part-timer to our long tenure
You be dork rhymer to our John Giorno
Yo, wisenheimer, who's your attorney
    ...some five-and-dimer
    who crashed your gurney?

Selves????

52

What's wrong widdat?
Representation! What a force!
Farce is the new representation!
Representation is the new farce!
Yeah! Visibility! What a force!
But we're invisible! What's left?
How Godot! And in the meantime?
And poiesis?
And polis?
Do I have to ask?
An overflowin' aesthetic?
But this flyover country ain't so fly!
Open like Olson or like Oppen?
            Or like Algarín?
A 24-7 poetics? When to sleep?
So can the ritmo undo the Gitmo?
Body as...site! Private or shared?
Mo' what?
Time-shared?
So where do we start?
What if we fester?
What's wrong widdat?
What's wrong widdat?
What's wrong widdat?

What's wrong widdis?
Representation? What a farce!
The new? What a farce!
You see!
Heh! Visibility's the new representation!
Invisible under god!
Inadvisable underdog!
As polis!
Poiesis half-assed!!
The answer, my friend, is overblowin'!
Exactly!
Yes, but the fly is open!

As in all-nighter!
Perchance to drum!
Algo...an algoritmo...
Go out and git mo'!
Mo' voice! Mo' body!
Slo-mo's OK!
With the commonest many!
Repeat it faster
Faster!
Faster!
What's wrong widdis?

communist manifesto

53

tomas de una siudad post-colapso

outtakes from a post-collapse siti

1.
no lleva "©" la "siti"
uno se sitúa
con tatuaje y sin estatus
en parques sin estatuas
sitizen sin estatuto
  "estates" disque "unite"?
disquiet estate!
un dáin no da a ten quid
ten cuidado, sitadino
estate quieto
no digas nada y dilo bien
no shoutouts for the wall st. crews
no bailouts no more
la siti owns these bancos
  (sin "©", tú sabes)
siéntate en ellos
son tuyos

1.
there's no "©" in "siti"
one sits
with tats and without status
in statueless parks
a statuteless *siudadano*
  "estates" as in "unite"?
¿bienes o raíces?
a dime? *¡no me digas!*
be careful, siti dweller
be still and chill
say nothing and say it well
tírale al corillo milla de oro
me late que no hay rescate ya
these benches are siti-owned
  (no "©," you know)
sit down on them
they're yours

2.
siéntate y siente
los murmullos
de la siudad sonriente
sin dientes
--mira, otro mendigo corporativo!
  (o sea CEO)
viene a pedir cuando ya no hay
sino la mella del animal situacional
que mira a la avenida y dice
  "la siti está mala"
y muele sus huesos
contra la acera
de veras
no me crees?
  "pues TiVo this!"

2.
sit down and feel
the murmurs
of the siti smiling
toothless
--look, another corporate panhandler!
  (CEO, that is)
he comes begging when there's nothing
but the plod of a situational animal
who stares at the avenue and says
  "it's bad in the siti"
and grinds his bones
against the sidewalk
for real
don't believe me?
  "well TiVo esto!"

3.

nunca hubo suelo nativo
ni aquí ni allá
sólo las carabinas las caravanas
las caras del caribe
grabadas en cruzacalles
que venden comunidades
      (*"empowerment zones"*)
y los texts bilingües en smartphones
anunciando campañas de concejales
que venden imunidades
con cejas gruesas y gafas grandes
      -¿qué ven desde sus siudades?
      -¿cómo se ve?
la siudad es panóptico sin lente
      -¿y cómo suena la canción
silente que nos une?
sibilante silabeante…
nuestro aliento es nuestro edén
           (*Pietri*)

3.

there never was a native soil
neither here nor there
only the carbines the caravans
the caribbean complexions
printed on billboards
that sell communities
      (*"comunidades especiales"*)
and the bilingual texts on smartphones
lobbying for councilmen
who sell immunities
with bushy eyebrows and big sunglasses
      -what do they see from their sities?
      -how does it look?
the siti is a lensless panopticon
      -and how does it go
that silent song we share?
in sibilant syllables…
our breath is our promiseland
           (*Pietri*)

4.

sucede que hay
diaspolíticas de mercado
poniéndole la "©" a la siti
la "©" de credit swap y de colonia
pero no procede
que se borre el sitibodi
y su sudor de isla
de lar sin legislar
somos la sede
      (no cede
        no cabe en un cd
        la cédula se disuelve)
sí, hay anuncios que nos sedan
      ("sedán del año")
con su ruido
      ("spring-fresh baño")
nos seducen con su estruendo
pero no reducen el sonido
de nuestro silencio
      ("hello darkness, miiii amiiiigo!")

4.

it so happens that there're
market diaspolitics
putting the "©" in siti
"©" as in colonial credit swap
but it doesn't follow
that one can erase the sitibodi
and its sweat of island
of unlegislated places
we are the site
      (no quit
        it won't fit on a cd
        the document's dissolved)
yes, there are ads that lull us
      ("this year's sedan")
with their noise
      ("mucho cling in your saran")
they seduce us with their ruckus
but they won't turn down the volume
on our silence
      ("hola darkness, viejo friend!")

¿cómo te digo?
nuestra sentencia es contar
(Ramos Otero)

¿se dan cuenta?
es llevar la cuenta en el cuerpo
sin deficit
de la presencia
de lo que somos
y lo que perdimos
de camino
a volver

how can I explain?
our sentence is our story
(Ramos Otero)

do you see?
it's keeping track on the bodi
without deficit
of the presence
of what we are
and what we lost
en route
to return

(*body slam*)

How many *días*
in your diaspora?
How many spores in
this melodía?
Viral, recombin-ante
repli-*cante*
sing the proles proliferative
zip-drived aggregate of cuerpos
bodies usb'd
(some still floppy from
the days of la colonia)
a colonography:
what else's there to write
since 1492?
what other site
a big hose up the new world's rear
qué rico!!
(not nearly as big as it thought it was)
exploratory surge
unperfumed, this colonia

Today to riposte
repost the founding text
as spam
as scoreless slam
to mic the font
to splay the layout
we're decibelletristes
of the bella y triste isla
that goes: Bx PR
mainland island
no X no PBR
only mainline to the vein
las venas demasiado abiertas

u no, tú sabej, glo-ball neo-gliberal
littoral with swinging doors
and rocking chairs with no committee
only derrieres al ritmo
del expect-a-culo
el óculo
the isle's panoptic
to rhyme in situ
to write the me-too

back in the '90s
Gómez-Peña rocked
the *border brujo*
but by now the brujos
are made-to-order
and the border sells at Borders™

*commodification
of
borderlands*

besides borders
aren't just metaphysics
or crossing sites
they're also the impasse
between bodies, the untouched skins,
unchecked assumptions, desires,
dreams of setting fire
to the self, the order,
the embrace

I propose a new border
not the incommensurable,
the trendy gap sold at The Gap™
all Muzak-souled
no, instead I call for the TM
not transcendental
but to i'm. the i.m.   possible tomorrow
the space between the TO (become)
and the MORROW/MARROW (contingent, provisional)
becoming's provision, that is what we are
islands in jet stream, always taking off
the skin between the T and the M
until we're empty, MT,
montanas out of mole
mellow mentes
funciones del ambiente (aplaude ahora)
speak fluent Torresian

58

almost Ambien™ but not quite
resisting
we keep the TM to ourselves
as subjects of colonia marked by trade
mark my tirade
we are the no-lony of colony
incólumnes
undoing the columns of calumny
re-siting the commons
no comma
cómo?

dotcomatose, the border corps
have trafficked, smuggled our transnation,
translocal are the bankers too
rob from the Bx and give to offshore tax dodge
getting bailed out
planting veiled doubts
that this is "our place" anymore
or ever was
can't spell "city" with a "y" these days
the "i" not Greek but Latin
as if to show they're "down wit"
Latin-nation (whoever that is)
whomever's datos
info-containment is the order of the day
buey, ecua-hey
but let's not talk about them
(olv-*idem*-os)
instead read these destellos
of no destiny except now
tu dei's tu moro
2pac a marrow
in one's pants
and scare the citizens
and rally the planets, no copay, compai
full coverage, in the wreckage
of discourse is the instant
the now não in all tongues
non-mono-ricua
mono a mono
the mono significante
knows no gates
negates as it affirms

and vice(tergi)versa
no can do!
craps! no dice! si dice!
I'm just sayin'
ahora es el momento
de decir
la hora de la dicha (bien o mal)
the minutest minuto
el sagging segundo
(minutemen in El Segundo?)
the instant without "in"
puro sin
puro stance
the national's relational
me late que
we're not too late for passion
fate's refashioning
pass ions to the body next to yours
charged, charred next to ours, hours
we're mute instruments
din from within
as energy, as instincts of a specious species
per di do en el es pa cio
es paz en el caos
is the "s" that never plurals
is the dry-erase mural
that remains
the shared singular of sing
the continente's ting
counting gente
cuenta en la cuneta y
canta
no cant
just
O!

II.

Let's make some noise
the semi-silent type
loud in its "yo is!"
"I soy!"
an otherwise non sequitur
(no sé quitarme de esto...
lo que es), no sequel
just the current playlist
the one attuned (I guess)
to the reggaetonal shifts
of barriles de bomba
juggling knots
juguetonal
nota to self:
no self today
except as analog
of Africa with looped tracks
those cyborg moves are so passé
like model burgs with moccafés
giving way to blisters, blight of blurbs
and remote servers in the exurbs
meanwhile here we do the dance
of the sí-borg in a no-burg
the no-bard in a sea of sí
come out meet your neighbors
your nosy, noisy neighbors
with their chismes ("noooo!" y "síííí!")
in that nosi dialectic
oral viral transmitter
the site's secretion
the moment matters as it's shared
the self's accretion
crawling to momentous shores
to plant the sí-no flag
(it is/isn't insignia'd)
supplant the empire's flags
with our sino unflagging
our casi-no royale
our people unflagged
the flagon's passed around

the streets and beachfronts
everyone drinks from it
its' not a PR or NY thing
or a dark horse trojan flogged on blogs
because we're all people of empires expired
we dance around their pyres
por ahora
because it's the now that matters
the no-e-si
the yo-a-ti
the poets-y
the moment muttered
and its amplified
composition by fields   of cane
americane
put the no in americano
so give it up for these hi-din sites
where polis leaks into the ether
(secret police go take a leak)
our secret's shared, is shard
charred word our hide
no hiding any longer
das ding of street
pump up the volumes of prose
and you still won't match these megahertz of silence
on mute trans/commute
mutations per metric foot
don't count just encounter
en contra-sentido
is what
we
do

III.

What we need here
is a body
a poetics
a bo-po
found, gestated, or prosthetic
the Bildung and its remains
the Dichtung and its domains
without a server, *non serviam*
no sirve, o sea
doesn't function
is defunct
but alive in its futility
in its spatiality
in its relation
(give up solo da funk)
to other pointless bodies
unencompassed, unbelonging

the oom-pah-pah of polka at the krump club:
somewhere here un papi con su drunk schlub persona
is drawing in the mamis (and their papis)
so boringly Freudian so ford-assembly-line macho
scratch that!
car song to myself instead:
i trans therefore i am
transambienting the iamb!

somewhere normaTIVO
is letting out its mating call
thru the digital wilderness
the bleat and gleam and beat of signal
but we're still here/hear
where the only poetics left
of where we are now is WE
we're left-of-center
square and its monuments
with no misgivings
(not giving it up for the MC's crew)
the toy timbales player takes a bow
laughtrack, rimshot

gold-toothed and arch, the McMC drops out and leaves
the stage to us
(no pro-tool'd *claves*)
going public with our freak, our glamguage
not our alterity (that goes
without saying)
but with what we go without
in our struggle to mean
something more than "We go"
to go not postal (*pos qué tal?*)
but post-declarative:

a post-declarative poetry wouldn't de-clare
(that is, it would make clear our no-clarity
de-familiarize the nuclear!
chloroform the clarion!
the carrion must fit under the beat in front of you!)
prescribing the Clearasil without the clear
the silliness comes through
(in other words pop it!)
just like Brasil (without the bra)
or Metamucil (be-mused meta-poetics?
you can keep Musil, Musiel, Muzak...)
and bring it back here to the ventana/sill of self
defenestrated
that is where the body's at
on the way down...
(like the krump club again?)
weighed down with "hoy" and "ahora"

give it up for the bodies of the moment!
the unrepresentative ones
but unrepentant
the cropped and crappy, crip and queer,
flopped and failing, flailing, hopeful ones
the ones that make the night what it is, our blessed ruin
the accentual eccentric music of biorhythm
toss the bio and the blurb
and touch the nerve
the very vervy/nervy/pervy verb:
volver: to return here, to meaning
(less the self?)
to ritual writ and un-
to the erratic wit

l'esprit raté du corps que expira...espérate...
(on flat rates with or without flatmates)
to float mute in the strata of bodies' dissolution
only to re-volver

we are what the mind makes
what the body allows
the cosmos and the chemistry
the error and the errancy
who knew these nomad particles,
this fragile circuitry?
never ending nerve endings:
irreverendings!
so what if today the body can't?!
no motion
social cues folded into the ambiento (sic)
that we still share
(the hugs minus the sinus)
death as daily affair
like orange and like orgasm
like sky and like sinew
like dross and floss
yet survival is daily

a poetics of the quotidian
would make the most of ether
(matter and its muttering)
no "either/or"
because bodies attract and repel
(Q: Is there another person?
A: None like you, each one another)
no one in particular
particle board of self
another evening's come
to this...what's left?

outside a fatal crash
on the front page:
spammed politics, e-newsletter
now the terms of fatalism are being rethought:
a hi-density conception of the self:
untracked and social
attract and set aside
adrift and usual in its meander

in its twisted figurations
thankfully too difficult to score — *music*
no dismount
only spectacle of skin
and our release from it
of sound and our rejoice in it
of pain and our response to it
appended to each other's story:
unreadable
no plot device
no *deus ex* in this machination
this rupture is our one way out
out two way in

the many ways that we begin
to make this music
this mawkish morning
when the storefronts should be closed
and the wounds should start to heal
today at last we are revealed
the shuffle of the city
finally becomes us

TICS (tongues)

(from the Spanish of César Vallejo)

I-

    King sitcom award for any they had
Scott Leslie Zaleski will get on the

    Local mosque to go to that is young
and one concept rather than them but I'm
easy enough that I'm a horror
take one last seen kick out enough zodiac
giving doesn't get it
innings without a cortisone
so what got us and I yell you to
           group by

  Vocal must go to ASU
you know in the wiki the season up out of the
      BUILDS MUSCLE IT ABUSED THEM WHEN THIS

    Yep means when a plastic
well spotted that I was on the imprint Africa
in the union work by the picky but you

II-

Dimple Dimple

Mint UBS bank island to entice
bone bubble lead on what they let chic
dimple D. and both he and opium will

Data Data

Dido scans the owner is co-bundle in buying
oh and I will be ethical to
a data in data and data

Montana Montana

There are also cutting them down and said
being such a say in the water coming out of
Magana Magana Magana Magana

Gnome but Gnome

Casey JAMA one police analysts
SingTel muddle me smoke about a sick
non-gnome but gnome buT

III-

    Trespass on us might notice
a gala award and
did I say since you will someday I will
yes, we'll school a

    Monitor the whole kennel them what I via

    Agony and not being a media in
    •   we help on the way
a cup on that bus out and gambles as Manlius
though the OS payments
classy and conceals local run people going to
get enough to sit on a dongle to Libya
Sudan is telephone Co.
MacOS X will suck enormous
Montevideo can know them what I via

    Channeled income of spinner by mostly in the
sabbaticals enemy was must pony to little us
on the squad is where most bullet assembly via
seen any evidence of what a sad
I'm it I limit also the Iowa East Coast
the Kabul steadily since a Magana

    What a sassy OEM to 16 minus
and if you don't we do it aside out real
do my daughter see him but in data is
downloading guy Silas McCain is
almost you can be emotional to us
                    not odious and most out of the

    Agony to not be needed near the
boost 1 pound payload of sporting a
number by now not to do how Lesotho
yet when he quarter Caruso said you

IV-

13 handles cut it us home to the US
asked on a B-three forecasts
when the moon got a seamless manner
Octavio Ossie the summer
I might well do we come to
photo one exhorted the West US
read us   to speak the rest

And the new zone was set up by the
must let out of the ghetto mambo sauce and
Sani Amico is a 40 or some in the
I'm okay to the city got us in my song
                                   Sunnydale's

Song was to see isotope equals to scuttles
you how to see network at the local
from their zone

I couldn't monitor this code I will
what not to level it out when this team we go to
eat your tool that comes young
what I can as you see us

How while you asked it comes by and see a
said you're a local   same data when I'll
and then I skew to

V-

Group will equal to your loan open ruler
this day is that there is pension is putting that
deny lexical names goal is to ideas
could you say how ugly I looks to it at all any that
group a little stalls appeared on this

A manner Octavio Seo seeing sediments
operator not fussy and dusty a Florida
EBM sings own than offset a child
he could only know sale beast the
nobody said anything adopts a

Lack and add levels said no kidding
Saddam might do to him what
you know Rios sentinel US entered me that
Westor Amazon that I think you need to
eatsale ticket at a combo
*by deployment at the Ottawa

I will will be cut at the Apple

VI-

In Hickey missed the manner
not a lot allow the need on data
Novell outlines will spray nozzle penis
and in total is song he or he know I
the atomicity don't have a
in that hate will be a post easier

Oligarchy and why he came by side was
and besides you just ignore
in the insult by him to my Aeschylus Les close us
then there thou go to bed am focused at me
told us my stung me ask
Army have a.
                    Do not own this will be that
at the Silas said Dallas goes to beginning up on that

Easy to PARC out of what ran
easy to be a vacuum in Nana and data
and they got him in a robust allow this decade
Palmdale as a game amendment that
sucking state check up we build what he he chose to
that robotic is a Saudi Casey for the
                    AMONG A LOT LATER
asked what I done to total two is Kaus

VII-

Croom basing nowhere that poor love it the ad like I did
gay dome is a goal boasting Obadiah
they made us he phoned they see a course SSE
each week a silo

But we guided more like a glass
this is a cycle and being Sunday the
Italy couple of idea that a decade in
it's keen on Eva not a Manlius

So Dumbo is not odious
AV block in a party that they got a low
by Russell medicine into flimsy ombre
                                        John!
One black-eyed days out of old Southwark with us
eBay going on the status got a slow Saturday is
just my men are less I listen those bogus

I'll without a miasma of fairness
sentiment was allowed less of me got us up in us
these boisterous East divided them
in my less blue for us I did close the Amiga was he imposed think you will know

VIII-

My man I is ultimately a when a
this identity I-95 Gopal there
in that ignited

My man at home via
city .pm touchup out of
own glad that they got appeals by Ahab
the company will host and single

We employ nothing that alloys
it only Montana seem in Nana
enter Los Gatos the game view than most
Mata hanged Espejo Atta
domed at the spots I need to appeal for them to
ask up at a dead vehicle
economic woman friendly CMS by the

IX-

    Old-school blues then or they voted been voted.
So for those of us I'm just sure what we
can say I'm an ancient wood and dataset Siong
then we could be a gamble I'm weekly peak of the
support is the own exciting to it by blessed
old lobby at that

    We'll school bluesman devoted they voted bit
asked what I will incapable anybody I announced I will see the this
I think Eagle Scout in this piece was once the abuse
17 done anal porn anal
so when I must been forced in the most almost fouled a
no people in bonus is Kaus and see a
            need in fact the

    Five doughboy who dared to go in the date when he
Wednesday debt in most Hamas in store also about NATO
they will use more yet in the lead of more than
this outliner
this levelheaded star
           Guam open a subhead as!

    EM but I said I limit it out was empty
    EM but I said I did money

X-

Peace Tina you we cannot be edited out in combat are
going to cacao by the more you
online might total to win every pension in seeing that
that is Mrs. Nelson EDS Lucy
only just been
meet travel more Octavio Lee

Well that that's the cell was young home tests
the own fabulous almost see him but S. Loma and what he smoked
out on the knee in the old lava at a

Or once autonomous by gayness up on Thomas
almost erase a stuff behind an equal
a week traveling to say I
on one of some animals guide Momo Thomas and Gus

Similarly the cabbie is Mrs. I see others in
I see all Thomas or to
go scaling portal may most bloody MPEG highness
Edelstein is Mrs. Bill since you
it is my babe is pension

Maligning you one of you and see a
  A. Busey and Bangor porosity
  B. he's in a room alone a donkey as these Buddhists

XI-

    Game won't travel many
in that ID e-mail that a silo
a case beset out of giving the euro he died he
not a lot reported that a

    If cleanliness me being a bully
any idea Nice Mono Sun and violence without
a worm by them I inevitable guileless glucose
deporting on East Muslim us he owned Mark Chelsea
                they salute and it also
                the nine coast boasts

        "Make Osvaldo,"
many say one but OKC most any nukes
in Goss out of the yummy form to
              say salvo
              satisfy the

    Database I knew it's definitely nice
given that it has gone national silo
there were houseboats of doom bass
go boldly and diagnose them go almost where

XII-

Is Koppel doing nothing that they will stop at US to
project the Indocid loan date act I
incident the only dumb although set of the guy look wooden Buddha

Just kill the most going game way to
a meet that this window each guy at the other
kinesiology with them
they ago not to resume in the postal costly sequence

Means that the only battle an Eskimo heat in
got each and the little of either
see what's been a sport without will
easy local portal to kick aside

XIII-

Penicillin POSIX so
seemed if he got a little cortisone beings went to sex the
I'm that he had a model will leave via
by the labeled long did he check is thanks a song
the more ratings in the knee in Columbia will
they handed I'll wouldn't say so

Beings went to six so so Thomas Prodi fecal
yet a morning also can be embedded in us home back
own gum with the own CV by
Dave feels me small
all clumsy and see a
young so see into but will believe it
terrible settlement Decatur bummed that whether

Always time that linea is the Oscar Willis
boys during the Lou*

Oldest random little!

compositional

3:42 pm

thought no more
than cloud

fence maybe

but still an opening

3:44 pm

temperatura
condición actual

sway

prior thought
was green too

does not erase

the marking
the scenery

3:46 pm

algae
is still
algo

so much
to consider
here

sunscape

the sky is scraped
some other way now

the way it never seemed
before

3:47 pm

resort communities
are everywhere

the ruin of this
after all

not the marshy pools

not the clouds

too close
for this late
in the day

3:49 pm

no pilot
in these palms

mic'd breezeway

hand-held devices
giving way

this vision

this stutter

3:52 pm

this spot

is also
private property

it matters in
as much as
shared

charred?

made public

texted
tested

like the story of these shores

3:54 pm

first Columbus

then the Americans
in 1898

go
global

return to
condition
of meaning

made
unmade

this waterlog

these puddles
of history

and i can see for Miles

12:21 pm

more than jetties
bridge of rock

algae, cacti
views in furious green

butterfly and gull
an easy tag-team somehow

here all makes
not sense but sentence

12:24 pm

asterisk shore
reminds of color

shorn
and recomposed

in dry

defying December

dismembering
the fine print of
memory

erased

12:56 pm

unresolved

feeling toward
the island

the coastline
in slow dissolve

the moorings
where to now?

the asking price is high
the expectations

these shores
shared how?

12:58 pm

what I've become
[...]
such a place now
[...]

1:00 pm

pained again
amid the cinders
is what the mind feels like

the smell here
like salt
[...]
not like December

1:01 pm

"If we make it through December"
the country song

this island knows no country
only songs

its elementary particles
sand and sorrow

sorrow and
stutter steps

the parting handshake
too slow to be repeated

1:03 pm

who let the dogs out
on the beach

no woofing, please
we're far too sick for that

but healing

the foam has that
effect on you

the famine too
of too much

too soon, tú sabes
tú y los tuyos

the discourse of experience

I yearn for this expanse

1:04 pm

let's contemplate
expulsion
from these territories

the oligarch's way is
paved with
seashells

bad checks
good times

stiff drinks

you know, lo usual

the unused
part of the self

is at the forefront here

the unseen frames
the scenery

we meet again
on our own terms, perhaps
or the sea's

desist

1:06 pm

the power's almost out my
apparatus

it appears I'm back to script now
back to voiced scrawl

the surplus is what scares me

the promise of unwriting
led me here

a leaden one
as with all promises

the sea

3:13 pm

after factotum

no scenery, sensoria

cacti green and coral blue

88

uvas de playa

uvular tubular and their synonyms

sounding like a cove

a covenant

the glare that we inhabit

these manglares

the word is meager mangled

now crash

the resolution

that is now

consignas para el fin del mundo

(2006)

En la ciudad de los museos feos todo el mundo quiere cantar tras los muros
y bailar en la claridad del seis sobrante
que truena en las aceras,
una puesta invertebrada sobre un mar de cadáveres:

Restos y ruinas, vientos azotando los semáforos colgantes,
las madres, el puño alzado en la plaza,
en la playa sin palmeras,
el alza de los precios del placer,
la sonrisa de aquel
que ha quedado de nuevo despierto
y desplazado.

Luz bélica, idilio en los escondites,
comadres en los comerciales,
alcaldías baldías, carritos de viandas
toboganiándose hacia el mismo devenir
de lo que fuimos y lo que somos
a la hora de la cena televisada.

Miedo, en medio de ciudades
de policías, reales y virtuales
simios al ataque, bajo techos estocados,
acechando, el viento deshace las persianas
de un dormitorio sin camareras.

"Aquel verano que crucé el Ponte Vecchio,"
dice la señora Aponte, y para de momento.

Es que la paridad social y el acceso a bienes
ya no es lo que era.

Lo que fue ya no es sino cieno tibio,
ínsulas baratarias, fango para adornar
los desfiles y las clínicas de familia
en las comunidades especiales.

Vaivén de palmeras, el sotto voce

apocalypse   **slogans for the end of the world**

(2009)

In the city of ugly museums everyone wants to sing behind the walls
and dance in the clarity of the surplus soul
that thunders on the sidewalks,
an invertebrate setting on a sea of cadavers:

Remnants and ruins, winds whipping the dangling stoplights,
the mothers, their fists raised in the square,
on the palm-less beach,
the rise in the price of pleasure,
the smile of the one
who's again been left awake
and displaced.

Light of war, idyll in the hideaways,
godmothers in commercials,
empty town halls, vegetable carts
tobogganing towards the same becoming
of what we were and what we are
in the hour of the televised supper.

Fear, in the middle of cities
of cops, real and virtual
apes on attack, under stuccoed roofs,
on the prowl, the wind undoes the window treatments
of a bedroom with no cleaning lady.

"That summer when I crossed the Ponte Vecchio,"
says Ms. Aponte, and stops all of a sudden.

It's just that social parity and access to goods
is no longer what it used to be.

What was is now no more than lukewarm murk,
islands on the trade route, mud with which to dress up
the parades and family clinics
in the empowerment districts.

Sway of palms, the sotto voce

del más reciente derroche mediático compartido
que les dio lugar a abogados agobiados
y alcohólicos leguleyos
que se escombran bajo umbrales
en las tardes lluviosas
en predios de cafetines.

Los productos de alto rendimiento,
cimiento y altiplano y
las antípodas construcciones—

      "Democracias, demos gracias
       a Mr. Crazy y su Gabinete"

Y los condómines
reunidos con sus dóminos
como aves de paso sin nidos,
de las que construyen
enjambres en las represas.

No, no es esa a la que me refiero.

Lo que digo es la ciudad en grado cero,
grosera, grande, degradada.
Inflada de hermosas miradas averiadas.
De multitudes peludas.
Donde nada se ha escrito.
Donde sólo se escribirá
el flujo desinhibido,
banal pero necesario,
de estar vivo de nuevo
en las capitales de ensueño,
injuriado y hogareño,
lejano y malsano.

Ni oboes y clarinetes.
Sólo ritmos sordos.
Ciudades de trasbordos.
Taburetes. Abarrotadas de datos
reales o insípidos.
nombres, números, nóminas.

La humanidad en perpetuo desalojo. En la ciudad sin estadios todos

of the latest shared media downfall
which gave way to frazzled lawyers
and alcoholic clerks
shrapneled under door frames
on rainy afternoons
in the vicinity of speakeasies.

The high-yield products,
foundations and high plains and
the antipodal constructions—

"Democracies, let us not forget
to thank Mr. Crazy and his Cabinet"

And the apartment-dwellers
huddled around their dominoes
like migratory birds without a nest,
the kind that build up
hives in dams.

No, that's not the one I mean.

What I mean is the city degree zero,
vulgar, big, degraded.
Inflated from the beautifully damaged stares.
From hairy multitudes.
Where nothing has been written.
Where all that will be written
is the uninhibited flux,
banal yet necessary,
of being alive again
in the capitals of dreamscape,
calumnied and homely,
distant and slow to heal.

No clarinets nor oboes.
Only deafening rhythms.
Transfer cities.
Footstools. Chock-full of factoids
real or insipid.
names, numbers, payrolls.

Humankind perpetually vacating. In the city without stadiums we are all

somos atletas. La estática intragable de los radios. Todos ganarán medalla de oro. Les llegará la hora a los voyeurs y las colegialas. Los cerrajeros y los gagos. Laureles para todos, con o sin papeles.

En el siglo diecinueve se idearon utopías, decimonónicas por definición. Pero hace rato que abandonaron en la esquina a ese antiguo catálogo de bogas.

Titulares de noticias: "El alza de los precios". "El costo de la guerra". "La huelga". "El subsuelo". "La supermodelo belga". "La Suiza transalpina". "La Galia y la ecolalia". "La ecología de la liberación". "Teleologías de izquierda". "Servicios contra la adicción". "Arresto encubierto". "En vivo desde Porto Alegre". "Logia masónica". "Blog amazónico". "Tres cuadrangulares". "Dio otro toletazo por tercera". "Abanicó a cuatro". "Hará sol en la cordillera". "Nocáut en el dogáut". "El disco de No Doubt". "El turismo cursi de vivir con convicciones". "Con Vicks". "Con visiones vaporrúbricas". "Edad mediata". "Vacuedad mediática". "Vaca asiática". "Sacra de los chakras". "Un panini exquisito". "La alquimia". "La auto-ayuda". "Las prácticas espiritualistas". "Los Poemas-Lista". "Listas para comer". "Comerse antes de comerciar". "Conversemos."

Montaje y desmontaje de ciudad. Ciudad-objeto imaginaria en su materialidad herniada. Fuente de canciones. La verdad telúrica del que ya no sueña, casi vacía la casa, el horno, las hornillas, cachivaches.

Auto-consciente del desasosiego de los Auto Parts en la carretera industrial que da a los suburbios posindustriales.

Doña Gloria toca la puerta siempreabierta de cierta casa desierta. La gata tuerta maúlla. Después de la trilla y la trulla quedan cenizas y vasos plásticos en el jardín.

Cada cual con su caneca. Gente escuálida se achueca (bien o mal) contra la cálida mueca del sol. Luz y laca y resaca y jaqueca y la paca de tecos que peca entre la pálida y la seca.

Discotecas de Tribeca. Tragan tragos y hacen amagos. Nuevos amigos en el ascensor. La misma podredumbre de costumbre. ¡Qué dolor! Tan felices juntos, como difuntos todavía no marchitos. Y las marchas por las avenidas, hoy por hoy venidas a casi menos que nada.

Discurso en las aldeas: la distorsión de voces micromegafónicas que piden paz para esta tierra que encierra a todos los que piden delante de los fotoperiodistas y diseñadores de sitios web.

Las tomas de sitio de la nueva sociedad—civil o no—que se va construyendo sobre el cruel gas lacrimógeno del ojo distópico que acota las derrotas de las uniones—civiles o no—
>   y las huelgas a medias
>   y las cortes de distrito
>   y resortes de detritus
>   y estrofas de distrofias.

athletes. The radios' static hard to swallow. All of them will win gold medals. The voyeurs' and the schoolgirls' time will come. The locksmiths' and the stutterers'. Laurels for all, with or without documents.

In the nineteenth century they came up with utopias, Victorian by design. But it's been a while now since they abandoned that catalog of vogues down by the corner.

News headlines: "The surge in prices." "The cost of war." "The strike." "The underground." "The Belgian supermodel." "The Swiss Alps." "The echolalic yelps." "The liberation ecologies." "The left-leaning teleologies." "The drug-prevention programs." "The undercover arrests." "Live from Porto Alegre." "Freemasons' lodge." "Amazonian blog." "Three home runs." "Hit another blast to third." "Fanned four." "It will be sunny in the mountains." "Knockout in the dugout." "The CD by No Doubt." "The mawkish tourism of living with convictions." "With Vicks." "With vaporubric visions." "Middling age." "Media vacuousness." "Asian cow." "Sacredest of chakras." "An exquisite panini." "The alchemy." "The self-help." "The spiritualist practices." "The List Poems." "Ready to eat." "Consume before commerce". "Let us converse."

Montage and dismantling of the city. Object-city imaginary in its herniated materiality. Source of songs. The teluric truth of the one who no longer dreams, the almost empty house, the oven, burners, bric-à-brac.

Self-conscious of the disquiet of the Auto Parts on the industrial road that leads to the post-industrial suburbs.

Doña Gloria knocks on the always open door of a certain deserted house. The one-eyed she-cat meows. After the ride and the parade there are ashes and plastic cups left in the garden.

To each his own rum flask. Squalid people (for better or worse) bump up against the sun's warm pucker. Light and lacker and hangover and headache and the pack of junkies that slip between the bad trip and the roach clip.

Tribeca discotheques. They swig drinks and make pretend. New elevator friends. The same old same old putrefaction. What a pain! So happy together, like the dead not withered yet. And the marches up and down the avenues, these days come to almost less than naught.

Speech acts in the villages: the distorsion of micromegaphonic voices that ask for peace for this land that encloses everyone who asks before the photojournalists and web designers.

The offsite outtakes of the new society—civil or not—that is getting built on the cruel tear gas of the dystopian eye that takes note of the defeat of unions—civil or not—
> and the middling strikes
> and the district courts
> and the detritus of spring
> and the dystrophied stanzas.

E insiste el Yo estofado u olvidado y sin sazón. Yo soy el estofón que canta como búho sobre esta sinrazón debajo de la axila.

Y las diatribas pueden más que los diatribadores

pero no más que las tribus montadas en el ómnibus que las lleva
a la gleba, a bañarse en la lava de las catedrales
a punto de estallar, diametralmente opuestas
a las cuestas que dan a los valles costaneros,
los derroteros derretidos y los ruidos del planeta
sin más treta que entregarse al trato hecho,
sin ángeles ni burdeles, sólo vestigios de litigios.

El prestigio de perder hace rato que ya lo hicimos nuestro. Vivimos del secuestro del poder hermoso del acoso a mano herniada.

¿Qué querrá decir semejante malestar? El elixir que no se deja tomar. La promesa que no se deja cumplir.

¡Qué amplio el parque
y la vista a la costa
y la hilera de columpios
y fuentes de agua
gris y metálica y
la verdad exílica
compartida por millones
de familias y naciones!

"Prefiero Montparnasse a Recoleta"
dice la Srta. Rodríguez-Gómez
con la cámara digital
al hombro y al escombro.

Planeta de ristras de turistas
e inmigrantes ilegales banales
en cuanto hermosamente reemplazables
como rehenes después de un armisticio.

Y en el tope de los edificios
          miles de manos empuñan sus ipods
y beben cerveza con sorbeto
          y hablan en balbuceos inquietos
sobre sus pasados de turistas e ilegales
          como compuertas las nubes se cierran

And so insists the I stuffed or set aside and unseasoned. I'm the bookworm who sings like an owl atop this underarm unreason.

And the diatribes are mightier than the diatribers

but not more than the tribes inside the bus that takes them
to the core, to bathe in the lava of the cathedrals
about to erupt, diametrically opposed
to the hills that lead to the coastal valleys,
the molten causeways and the planet's noise
without a ruse, just done-deal surrender,
no angels and no brothels, only vestiges of quarrels.

The prestige of losing we made ours long ago. We live off of the abduction of the beautiful power of pursuit at stunpoint.

What might such malaise all mean? The elixir that won't let itself be swallowed. The promise that won't let itself be kept.

How vast the park
and the view of the coast
and the row of swings
and water fountains
gray and metallic and
the exilic truth
shared by millions
of families and nations!

"I prefer Montparnasse to Recoleta"
says Miss Rodríguez-Gómez
with the digital camera
on her shoulder asmolder.

A planet of tourist strands
and banal illegal immigrants
banal as in beautifully replaceable
like hostages after an armistice.

And on the tops of buildings
          thousands of hands clench their ipods
and sip beer with a straw
          and speak in restless babblings
about their pasts as tourists and illegals
          like floodgates the clouds close in

sobre la luna menguante
      y en el penthouse que da al río
el libre albedrío de las horas
      corre su desconcertante curso.

El hurto de la noche ya es completo:
encapuchada, asfixia a los señores con gabanes caros pero inocuos
y a sus hijos de tedio taciturno y a las abuelas con pechos mentolados.

Ha llegado la hora de alejarse o acercarse al exorcismo (que es lo mismo que seguir
parodiándose a uno mismo. Como antropos jugando a los topos en la calle con urgencia casi
carcelaria.)

Y es que después de los museos
quedan reos, risas, nebuleos,
cuadros y recuadros y pasillos
y estatuas y atriles y lienzos
y viejos comienzos
y niños comiéndose la cuerda floja,
el hilo discursivo
que nos une, umbilical,
igual a los museos,
a la musa ilusa
que es más cara que decir:

"Somos museos,
      usémosnos
           para poner cuadros
y recuadros;
      seamos Prometeos
           coetáneos
de la crisis
      en esta fiesta a cuestas
           subiendo
de piso en piso
      de zona en zona
           a la luz de la duda yuxtapuesta
como un periodista
      despedido
           dormitando al mediodía
debajo de un faro
      en época de guerra
           apuntalando los disparos
y sus melodías internas

around the waning moon
        and in the riverfront penthouse
the freewill of the hours
        runs its disconcerting course.

The night's theft is now complete:
hooded, she suffocates the sirs with expensive yet innocuous suits and their tediously taciturn
sons and grandmothers with mentholated chests.

The time has come to drift away or to approach the exorcism (which is the same as to keep on
parodying oneself. Like anthropos shooting craps out on the street with an almost prison-
worthy urgency.)

And it's just that after the museums
there are still culprits, laughter, hustle,
pictures and insets and hallways
and statues and lecterns and canvases
and old beginnings
and children snacking on the tightrope,
the discursive thread
that joins us, umbilical,
the same as the museum,
to the clueless muse
that costs us more than saying:

"We are museums,
        let's use ourselves
                to put up pictures
and insets;
        let us be Prometheuses
                coetaneous
with the crisis
        in this party scarred
                going up
floor by floor
        zone by zone
                by the light of nearby doubt
like a journalist
        laid off
                dozing off at midday
under a lighthouse
        in wartime
                shoring up the gunshots
and their inner melodies

deseando de repente
        bailar de nuevo
entre tanta gente
      en la claridad del sol que arde
         aún".
              Y son las dos y veinte
de la tarde.

wishing suddenly
           to dance again
among so many people
        in the clarity of the sun blazing
              still."
                    And it's two-twenty
in the afternoon.

———————

Urayoán Noel is the author of the book/DVD *Kool Logic* (Bilingual Press, 2005) and two collections of poetry in Spanish: the object-book *Las flores del mall* (2000) and *Boringkén* (2008). A contributing editor of *Mandorla,* he is the translator of the chapbook *Belleza y Felicidad* (Belladonna, 2005), and has translated a variety of Latin American and U.S. Latino/a poets. His reviews and essays have appeared in *Contemporary Literature*; *BOMB*; and *Diasporic Avant-Gardes* (Palgrave), and he has performed internationally, both solo and as part of Spanic Attack. Originally from San Juan, Puerto Rico, Noel divides his time between the South Bronx and upstate New York. He teaches English at the University at Albany, SUNY, where he is a faculty advisor to the online poetics journal *Barzakh*.

Made in the USA
Charleston, SC
08 September 2015